The Majesty of the

MISSISSIPPI DELTA

Text by Jim Fraiser

Photography by West Freeman

Foreword by John C. Willis

PELICAN PUBLISHING COMPANY
Gretna 2002

For my mother, Adelyn Gerald Stokes;
my mother-in-law, Terry Draughn Sullivan;
and their beautiful granddaughters, Lucy
and Mary Adelyn—J. F.

For my wonderful wife, Aimee Adatto Freeman
and my fabulous children,
Alexandra, Andrew, Ella, and Scott—W. F.

Text copyright © 2002
By Jim Fraiser

Photographs copyright © 2002
By West Freeman

Library of Congress Cataloging-in-Publication Data

Freeman, West.
   The majesty of the Mississippi Delta / photography by West Freeman ; text by Jim
Fraiser ; foreword by John C. Willis.
     p. cm.
   ISBN 1-56554-869-8 (alk. paper)
     1. Architecture—Mississippi—Delta (Region)—19th century. 2.
Architecture—Mississippi—Delta (Region)—20th century. I. Frasier, Jim, 1954- II. Title.

NA730.M72 D454 2002
728'.37'09763309034—dc21

                                                                2001052075

Printed in Korea
Published by Pelican Publishing Company, Inc.
1000 Burmaster Street, Gretna, Louisiana 70053

Contents

Landmarks of a Bygone Age 5
Acknowledgments 7
The Yazoo-Mississippi Delta 9
Gateway to the Delta 11
    Port Gibson 11
    Windsor 12
    First Presbyterian Church 13
Vicksburg 14
    Annabelle 15
    Cedar Grove (Klein House) 18
    The Corners 20
    Balfour House 22
    Willis-Cowan Home (Pemberton's Headquarters) 24
    Warren County Courthouse 26
    Floweree 27
    Vicksburg National Military Park 30
    The Bobb House (McRaven) 31
    Anchuca 34
Rolling Fork and Vicinity 36
    Mount Helena 37
Yazoo City and Vicinity 39
    No Mistake Plantation 40
    The P-Line House 42
The Heart of the Mississippi Delta 44
    LAKE WASHINGTON VICINITY 44
        Ruins of St. John's Episcopal Church 45
        Junius B. Ward House (Erwin House) 46
        Mount Holly 47
        Linden 48
    GREENVILLE 49
        The First National Bank Building 50
        St. Joseph Roman Catholic Church 51
        Hebrew Union Temple 52
        Griffin-Spragins House (Refuge Plantation) 53

Belmont 54
GREENWOOD 56
Historic Cotton Row District 57
Lusco's 58
Leflore County Courthouse 59
River Oaks 60
Bridgewater Inn 62
Revelee (The Gwin House) 64
Carter House 66
Provine House 68
Grand Boulevard Historic District 70
Bellashon 71
Bledsoe House 74
Rosemary 76
Jones House 78
CLEVELAND AND VICINITY 81
Isaiah T. Montgomery House 82
CLARKSDALE 83
The Clark Mansion 84
The Cutrer Mansion 85
Wildberger House 86
Madidi Restaurant 87
ENDURING DELTA INFLUENCE 88
Ole Miss (The University of Mississippi) 88
Lyceum Building 89
Barnard Observatory 90
Rowan Oak (William Faulkner's Home) 91
Ventress Hall 92
HOLLY SPRINGS 93
Walter Place 94

Landmarks of a Bygone Age
John C. Willis

Water and soil, soil and water—these elements have played crucial roles in the development of the Yazoo-Mississippi Delta. It was water that carved out the alluvial plain, water that carried rich silt down the course of the Mississippi River with every flood over a millennium, and water that retreated to leave behind a rich topsoil. That soil—thick, stone-free, and fecund—drew a steady influx of immigrants to the region in the nineteenth century, hopeful thousands from Asia, South America, Europe, and North America, as well as involuntary settlers brought from Africa in chains. Overcoming challenges from flood, war, epidemics, and the boll weevil, these settlers remained in the region and transformed it from wilderness into a prosperous farming area. Indeed, the Delta became King Cotton's prize domain. By the 1880s, U.S. government reports publicized what many agriculturists had suspected for decades—that the Delta contained the world's highest proportion of plant food in its soil. Upon this soil, and despite the flood-prone Father of Waters' propensity to take away as much as he gave, a plantation empire dedicated to cotton production emerged and prospered.

But the region's story is not a linear tale of ever-increasing achievement. There have been times when the course of Delta history was unpredictable, even retrograde. Although anthropologist, folklorists, historians, and travel writers frequently employ the Delta as a symbol for the larger South, the sub-region's experiences have often been at odds with the region it is forced to represent.

Many times, the Delta has been portrayed as something it wasn't: vital to the Old South. For example, *The Majesty of Mississippi Delta* reveals that much of northwest Mississippi possessed only the slimmest antebellum tradition. The alluvial plain north of Vicksburg was still ninety percent wilderness when the Civil War broke out. Most of the improved land and settlements stood along the Mississippi River, beside its major tributaries, or upon the broad natural ridges raised a few feet above flood level. The Delta's vast interior stood unchanged by the hand of man. Myriad varieties of oak, gum, cypress, and cottonwood rose up out of the fertile soil, and thick canebrakes choked its "open" places. And by 1865, even the tenuous outpost of settlements beside rivers or upon ridges were threatened by inundation or the creeping expansion of the forest. The depredations of rival armies and the depletion of the labor force made it difficult to keep levees, fields, ditches, fences, barns, and homes in good repair. In sum, the Delta remained in the shadows of the Old South, and was more obliterated by the Civil War than many better-known areas.

Too, the region has often been ignored or forgotten for what it truly was, especially in the period after the Civil War. Looking back, the twentieth century, when the Delta attracted many writers and photographers eager to chronicle and assess its business plantations, the region's past seemed dominated by broad fields and big houses. Its African-American majority, comprising up to eighty percent of the population, seemed consistently shackled by poverty and limited horizons, even decades after emancipation. Not realizing how close

Delta landowners came to bankruptcy in the wake of the Civil War, these observers could not guess how far the region's planters had stretched to gain freed laborers and land buyers. Realizing they might lose all their holdings, white landowners of the late nineteenth century offered surprisingly lenient rental terms to former slaves who would move to the thick-forested interior and clear and cultivate those acres in cotton. Rental fees from these tenants—and it was renters, not sharecroppers, who dominated the ranks of non-owning Delta farmers until 1910—helped landlords save, maintain, and expand their riverside holdings.

Thus, at the close of the nineteenth century the Delta presented two faces: along the major ridges and rivers a plantation district thrived, while in the interior, black farmers elected black officials and traded with black merchants. By 1900, African Americans comprised two-thirds of the Delta's farm owners, and the region was a promised land for small farmers across the South. But this era of balanced prosperity and divergent opportunity was overturned by improvements in the cotton market and the arrival of the boll weevil. By 1920, large plantations had spread into the region's interior. Landlords expressed a strong preference for sharecropping laborers instead of renters and the African Americans' climb up the agricultural ladders was haulted, then reversed.

Those who use the region as only a symbol of the South have largely overlooked the Delta's era as a land of opportunity. Its successful black farmers inhabit a forgotten time. Except for Mound Bayou, the generations of aspirant African Americans left few physical monuments to their efforts. By contrast, rising planters and merchants created numerous structures along the riversides, some in heroic styles and exotic stones, others in shapes and materials more reflective of the region's climate and resources. Their influence spread into the interior, along with their homes, businesses, and architectural preferences. Now, apart from the expansive fields, there is little architectural difference between the old-time plantation districts and the once wild interior.

Nor are there many tangible reminders of the region's tumultuous nineteenth-century history, save the houses, commercial buildings, and the monuments considered in this volume. Jim Fraiser and West Freeman deserve our thanks and appreciation for their work in representing these landmarks of a bygone age. For the structures considered in these pages have stood against the water, laid claim to the soil, and sheltered and inspired the men and women whose ambitions and disappointments at which we can only guess.

—JOHN C. WILLIS

Acknowledgments

We are most grateful to Richard Cawthorn, Chief Architectural Historian for the Mississippi Department of Archives and History, whose assistance to the authors and dedication to the preservation and documentation of historic Mississippi sites and structures has been invaluable to this project.

We would also like to thank Bill and Mary Jayne Whittington, Suzy Gordon, Tim Kalich, Wyatt Emmerich, George and Carolyn Mayer, S. J. Tuminello, Hugh McCormick, Drick Rogers, Mr. and Mrs. Jim Rushing, Hayes and Carolyn Dent, Allen Spragins, Virginia O'Neal, Meredith McBee, Carol Ann Adams, Hal Fiser, Jorja Lynn, Judge John Fraiser, Martha Fraiser Bryant, Mr. and Mrs. John Sullivan, Mr. and Mrs. Robert Montgomery, Bobby and Juanita Baker, John C. Willis, Chief Phillip Martin, Carole Fraiser, Aimee Freeman, Richard and Sandra Freeman, Tina Freeman, Be-Be and Ken Adatto, and Professional Color Service (who did all of the E-6 processing for West's film). Also we thank all the homeowners who allowed us to photograph their lovely homes and gave us the pleasure of their company because without them this book would have never happened, and also Nina Kooij, Cynthia Williams, and Dr. Milburn Calhoun for their much-needed aid and support.

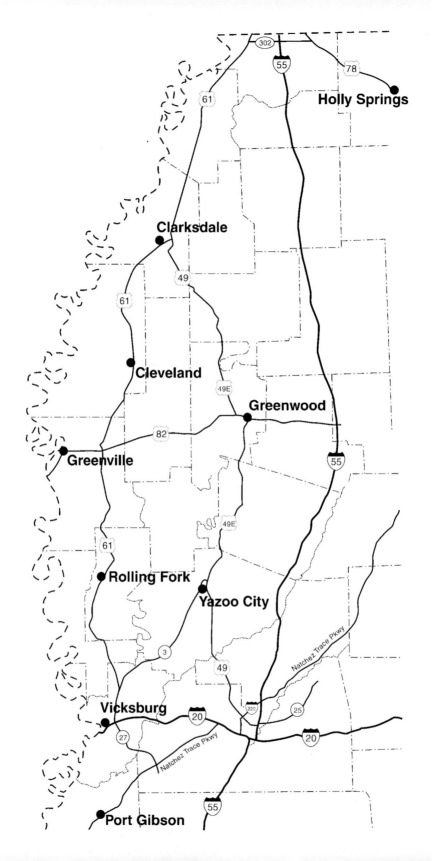

The Yazoo-Mississippi Delta

The region commonly referred to as the "Mississippi Delta" is a fifty-two-mile-wide, two-hundred-mile-long, flat, alluvial plain formed by millennia of silt deposits from the flooding of the Mississippi and Yazoo Rivers. It is bounded by the Mississippi River on the west, the Loess Bluffs to the east, Memphis to the north, and Vicksburg to the south.

Technically speaking, however, this region is actually the Yazoo-Mississippi Delta, since the actual Mississippi Delta is where the Mississippi pours into the Gulf of Mexico, south of New Orleans. But then, why should anyone expect the "Mississippi Delta" to lend itself to any precise title or explanation, when the region itself is so many things to so many people?

For the more historically minded, it's the setting for several key Civil War battles and the locale where President Theodore Roosevelt turned down a chance to shoot a helpless bear cub, an act that led to the invention of the world-famous child's toy, the teddy bear.

To others, the Delta is all about agriculture, from the ubiquitous cotton plantations to other agrarian experiments such as rice paddies, corn and soybean fields, and the most recent development, catfish farms. For still others, the Delta brings to mind Las Vegas-style casinos, abundant fish and game, or the white-columned mansions made famous by Hollywood filmmakers.

For our purposes, though, there is yet another aspect of the Delta that warrants consideration. This is the region's architecture, which—like its history, land, and people—helps to explain what the Delta is all about. And perhaps more so than in any other American region, the Delta's architecture has been forged by the region itself.

For example, the Delta's constant flooding encouraged the construction of raised houses and cottages, not only so the inhabitants could stay high and dry during inundation, but also so home owners could slip logs under their houses and roll them away from the river's deadly encroachment. The oppressive summertime heat and humidity led to higher ceilings with taller windows, dogtrot hallways and second-floor galleries, all of which gave access to mercifully cool breezes. The balconies also served a second purpose of shading first-floor windows, doors, and walls. The near-tropical rains gave rise to the use of steep-hip roofs for drainage, and gutters and cisterns for essential water

Delta mansion overlooking plantation fields.

collection. And when King Cotton raised his scepter of prosperity in the early twentieth century, the people erected mansions with majestic Greek columns, gigantic triangular pediments, intricately-designed windows, fancy cornices and doorways, and such other displays of wealth and ostentation as architecture could devise.

Ingrained in the Delta's architecture are history, devotion, pretension, honor, and avarice. And it is there that we find a lasting testimonial to man's ingenuity in the face of nature's constant attempts to dislodge, discomfort, or destroy him.

Newly planted Delta cotton field viewed from atop a levee.

Gateway to the Delta

Port Gibson

The traveler heading north on Highway 61 from Natchez gets an inkling of what lies ahead in the Mississippi Delta when entering Port Gibson, a cotton town located directly across the Mississippi River from Louisiana's plantation country. Founded in 1788 by beekeeper and planter Samuel Gibson, this hamlet on the river's bluffs offers all the faded beauty, flamboyant quirkiness, and antebellum splendor that the Delta tourist expects. The haunting ruins of Windsor, the eccentric hand atop the steeple of the First Presbyterian Church, and the grandeur of Oak Square—a house that cotton built—are among the treasures of Port Gibson that let the sojourner know that there's something magical just up the road in Mississippi's Delta.

St. Joseph's Catholic Church (Church & Coffee Streets) was built in 1863 by Elvie Bowie Moore, the niece of the frontiersman Jim Bowie, in large part to provide for the spiritual needs of parishioners' slaves.

Windsor
Near Port Gibson off Highway 552

Twenty-two of the original twenty-nine, thirty-foot-high, fluted, stucco-over-brick columns, with iron Corinthian capitals are all that remain of the glory that was once Windsor. Built with slave labor by Smith Coffee Daniel, II, at a cost of $175,000, the sixty-five-square-foot raised Greek Revival mansion with twenty-three rooms was once mistaken for a college by riverboat pilot Mark Twain.

Confederates used Windsor as an observation post during the Civil War, sending lamp signals from its cupola across the Mississippi River to Louisiana. Daniel's wife, Catherine, saved it from destruction by federal troops by allowing them to use it as a Union hospital in 1863, only to have it razed on February 17, 1890 by an accidental fire started by a discarded cigarette.

Eight surviving columns of Windsor, southwest elevation. The ruins are listed on the National Register of Historic Places (1971).

First Presbyterian Church
Corner of Walnut and Church Streets (Highway 61)

Architect James Jones built the Gothic Revival-style First Presbyterian Church in 1859 for Rev. Zebulon Butler, only to have Butler's funeral serve as the church's first official service a few months later. Butler had zealously opposed slavery in the 1850s and had succeeded in sending 300 slaves back to their African homelands. So popular was Butler with his congregation that they erected a wooden hand atop the church's spire in memory of his finger-raising sermons.

The wooden landmark was so well attended by woodpeckers that the five-foot-long finger fell off in 1905 and was replaced with the present twelve-foot-long metal hand. The church still has its original slave gallery and a chandelier from the famous steamboat, "Robert E. Lee."

First Presbyterian Church, west elevation, with its clenched hand and finger pointing heavenward, so inspired Gen. U.S. Grant during his 1863 occupation of Port Gibson, he declared the town to be "too pretty to burn."

"The Mississippi Delta begins in the lobby of the Peabody Hotel in Memphis and ends on Catfish Row in Vicksburg."   —*David L. Cohn*

Vicksburg

Some question the accuracy of associating Vicksburg with the nearby Delta flatlands, aware as they are that in 1790 the Spanish treasured it for its easily-defended hills, a topography that ultimately led to its early American name, Walnut Hills, and its enduring nickname, the Bluff City. But flatness by itself does not make the Mississippi Delta. The Delta is also state of mind, and a mind whose foremost consideration has always been cotton.

Not long after Methodist minister Newitt Vick arrived from Virginia in 1814 and founded Vicksburg, cotton became the primary agricultural staple. In the 1830s, Vicksburg became the chief export point for the Delta's expanding cotton empire. Oxen-drawn wagons, pole-driven flatboats and Yazoo River steamboats brought interminable payloads of white gold to Vicksburg, whose people grew wealthy from the trade.

Wealthy enough, history relates, to subdue rioting riverside gamblers in 1835, survive devastating tornados and floods on a near-annual basis, endure the worst wartime siege on American soil in 1863, and engineer their way around the Mississippi River's 1876 attempt to bankrupt them by abruptly changing its course and leaving Vicksburgers without a river at the base of their bluffs for twenty-five lean years.

The Mississippi River Bridge at Vicksburg was named to the National Register of Historic Places in 1989.

Annabelle

501 Speed Street

John A. Klein built this house in 1868 for his son, Madison Conrad Klein. The arched front windows, including the three-sided bay window with two-over-two double-hung sash, and the asphalt gable roof with a cross gable over a two story projection, reveal Annabelle's Victorian-Italianate style. The one-story front porch is covered with cast-iron columns and features an ornate, dentiled cornice supported by paired brackets.

A 1953 tornado carried away the original roof, but George and Carolyn Mayer restored Annabelle in 1992, adding bathrooms and electricity and furnishing their residence with European art and antiques handed down through four generations of the Mayer family.

Annabelle, south elevation. Adjoining the main structure is a Queen Anne guesthouse complex built in 1881.

Annabelle's dining room, furnished with a ten-piece centennial Chippendale table and chairs made of ribbon mahogany. The china cabinet and buffet are original pieces. The clock is of 1804 French Empire vintage.

Annabelle's front parlor is lighted by an Italianate, three-bay window. A rare Victorian piano desk, with secret hiding places, is on the right.

A 1780 William and Mary cock-fighting chair was fashioned of oak and walnut.

Early 1700s Boulle ladies writing desk, or bonheur du jour, is of ebony veneer and inlaid with tortoise shell and brass.

Cedar Grove (Klein House)

2200 Oak Street

Virginian jeweler and clockmaker John Alexander Klein moved to Vicksburg in 1836 to take advantage of the town's prime commercial location on the Mississippi River. In 1840, he built Cedar Grove as a brick, two-and-one-half-story, Greek Revival residence with New Orleans-style cast-iron galleries, cypress floors, floor-to-ceiling windows, Italian marble fireplaces, and four Tuscan columns sheltering front and rear elevation balconies. Klein made additions in 1852 of south and north wings, and in 1870 of a bracketed bay window to provide more space for his wife, Elizabeth Bartley Day, and their ten children. Klein eventually became known as the "Prince of Commerce" for achieving success as a banker, lumber baron, railroad magnate, and Delta cotton plantation owner.

Named for the ancient, majestic, cedar trees on its grounds, the mansion escaped major damage during the forty-seven-day siege of Vicksburg, thanks to the influence of Elizabeth's cousin, Union Gen. William T. Sherman. Even so, Cedar Grove was the first house fired upon by the federal armada in 1863, an assault which left two cannonballs lodged in a front parlor wall and floor. Cedar Grove was listed on the National Register of Historic Places in 1976 and is open to the public as a tour home and guesthouse.

Cedar Grove, west (front) elevation, with its lavishly-decorated sixty-plus rooms, is one of the South's largest and most opulent antebellum mansions.

The ballroom, built in 1850, with original flooring, an 1876 centennial grand piano, Italian harp, Regina music box, French pier mirror, and gas-burning chandelier. As many as thirty-five couples danced the Quadrille, Polka, and Reel in this room. The ladies attached a dance card to their wrists with a ribbon, which the gentlemen signed in order to reserve certain dances for themselves.

The Kleins' master bedroom, with original Mallard armoire and baby bed, Italian marble fireplace, French mirror, Episcopalian "prayer chair," carved rosewood dressing table, and the original canopied bed in which General Grant slept while intoxicated after the siege. The room is now a bed and breakfast that may be rented overnight.

The Corners
601 Klein Street

John A. Klein designed and built The Corners in 1873 as a wedding gift for his daughter, Susan, who married Capt. Isaac Bonham of the Seventh Virginia Cavalry in the spring of that year. Bonham was accidentally killed in 1883 while attending a duel, but the home remained in the Klein family for decades.

This brick, raised cottage features a mixture of architectural styles, including Rococo Revival interior plaster decoration, a Victorian gallery with Italianate paired brackets supported by eleven rectangular gingerbread columns inlaid with decoratively-sawn panels, Italianate cornices above side windows, and a Greek Revival frontispiece with wide overhanging cornice, and full-length, square-headed nine-over-nine windows.

The Corners' geometric brick walks, parterre gardens, enclosing cast-iron fence and brick-lined gutters are all original, as are the rear slave quarters and the dining room cupboards with butterfly shelves. The sixty-eight-foot-long front porch affords an excellent view of the Yazoo-Mississippi river basin.

The Corners, west elevation, is listed on the National Register of Historic Places (1977).

The Corners' master bedroom is decorated Victorian style and features a canopied Mallard bed.

Balfour House

1002 Crawford Street

"As I sat at my window, I saw mortars from the west passing entirely over the house and the parrot shells from the east passing by-crossing each other, and this terrible fire raging in the center."

So reads the famous Civil War diary of Emma Balfour, the mistress of Balfour House, who, if peering out her front window, could have seen the Sisters of Mercy scurrying about their front yard ministering to wounded Confederate soldiers or observed officers hurrying in or out of General John Pemberton's Confederate Headquarters, next door.

During the Christmas season of the previous year, she and her husband William had been hosting a gala ball at their two-story, red brick, Federal and Greek Revival home—the ladies in their fancy gowns and the youthful officers in their Confederate grey, having just formed separate lines to dance the Virginia Reel—when the general in charge of Vicksburg's defenses suddenly arrived at their Corinthian-columned doorstep with word that Yankee gunboats were swiftly approaching. "This ball is at an end," he announced.

Undaunted by continuous Union shelling and refusing to reside in a cave as did so many of her neighbors, Mrs. Balfour remained in her home throughout the siege, taking in wounded soldiers and sending buttermilk to Gen. Stephen D. Lee and his staff every morning. To her chagrin, July the Fourth found Balfour House serving as Union Gen. James B. McPherson's headquarters following Vicksburg's capitulation.

Balfour House, south elevation, was built in 1835 by William Bobb and acquired by the Balfours in 1847. It is listed on the National Register of Historic Places (1979).

This three-story, elliptical, spiral staircase features all original wood, including twenty-five cypress steps on each floor and a mahogany handrail atop square spindles.

Federal-style wallpaper with swags and gargoyles in the border and a painting of Emma Balfour grace this front parlor, along with an 1872 rosewood Chickering piano. The central hall door casings are treated architecturally with fluted Ionic pilasters supporting a well-proportioned full entablature.

Willis-Cowan Home (Pemberton's Headquarters)
1018 Crawford Street

Built in 1836 by Martha Vick Willis, the daughter of Vicksburg's founder Rev. Newitt Vick, the Willis-Cowan Home is a National Historic Landmark. But this rectangular form, narrow-columned Federal-style house with an unmistakable Grecian flair (a two-tiered porch with square posts and a full entablature with Ionic columns and pilasters added in 1851) is more famous for having served as Lt. Gen. John C. Pemberton's Confederate Headquarters during most of the forty-seven-day siege of Vicksburg. It was here that Pemberton made the fateful decision to surrender the town on July 3, 1863, an act that many Southerners believe accounted for the necessity, decades later, of having a local priest perform an exorcism to rid the house of lingering demons.

Current owner A. J. Johnson renovated the house from 1997 to 1999, preserving many original window panes; all nine fireplaces, some with original unpainted cypress mantles and chimney closets; the slate roof, and an elegant stairway leading to the second floor. Johnson also restored the original colors to every interior wall and added bathrooms to each of the five upstairs rooms.

Pemberton's Headquarters, south elevation, was struck many times by enemy shells; one cannonball remains embedded in the east parlor floor.

This original Federal-style curved staircase rises from a center hall that was once a porch, so the cypress flooring is slanted for running off water. The stairsteps are made of pine and the handrail is walnut. The window panes above the pocket doors are also original. The room's walls have been restored to their original colors.

Warren County Courthouse
1008 Cherry Street

   Designed by William Weldon and built of handmade brick by slave labor in 1858, this courthouse museum is a National Historic Landmark, housing one of the South's largest and best collections of Civil War and Native-American artifacts. It is also architecturally outstanding, with its original iron doors and shutters and four porticos supported by thirty-foot-tall, fluted Ionic columns situated at each of the four entrances.

   Jefferson Davis launched his political career here, and Presidents Zachary Taylor, U. S. Grant, William McKinley, and Theodore Roosevelt also spoke here. From the open-domed cupola, Confederate generals watched their ironclad Arkansas single-handedly take on the Union fleet and later decided to house Union prisoners in the courtroom to discourage federal shelling.

In 1978, the Greek Revival-style Warren County Courthouse (east elevation) was selected by the American Institute of Architects as one of the twenty most outstanding courthouses in America.

Floweree

2309 Pearl Street

When civil war erupted in 1861, Charles C. Floweree was enrolled at the Virginia Military Institute. He promptly joined the Seventh Virginia Infantry Regiment and saw action at the battles of Bull Run (First Manassas) and Seven Pines. At the age of twenty, he took part in Pickett's fateful Gettysburg charge, and was promoted to colonel shortly thereafter, the youngest Confederate ever to gain that rank. After capturing a Union general and four hundred troops at the Battle of Drewry's Bluff, Virginia, Floweree himself was captured in 1865 and held at Johnson's Island for the remainder of the war.

Colonel Floweree moved to Vicksburg in 1866, where he married Jennie Wilson, whose father brought him into the family ice business. In 1877 his wife received the deed to a parcel of John A. Klein's estate, on which Floweree built the townhouse that now bears his name. Reputed to have been constructed by Bavarian immigrants, the home was crafted in the Victorian-Italianate style, as evidenced by its double-bracketed eaves, massive frontispiece, and heavy segmentally-arched openings.

In 1961, the present owner, architect S. J. Tuminello, replaced a deteriorating portico of clustered wooded columns with a robust portico of square, paired-brick columns. A semi-octagonal breakfast room replaced a former kitchen in 1971.

Floweree, west elevation entrance, was included on the National Register of Historic Places in 1975.

Floweree's dining room ceiling decoration is enriched with chandelier medallions of elaborate plasterwork of the "High Victorian Age" rococo phase. The marble mantle was designed with a characteristic Italianate, arched opening.

The front parlor plasterwork decorating the ceiling and the arch of the bay window consists of an elaborate program of richly-designed medallions, cartouches and moldings.

The Victorian guest bedroom has a canopied Mallard bed and a high ceiling, characteristic of Floweree.

Floweree's windows, like this one in the guest bedroom, were created with rare joinery skill, evidenced from the louvered blinds surrounded by wide architraves with rolled backbands.

Vicksburg National Military Park
Clay Street near I-20

The Siege of Vicksburg lasted from May 18 to July 4, 1863, during which time beleaguered citizens lived in caves to avoid hourly shelling and dined on mules and rats to escape starvation. Prior to the siege, the Confederates had handily repulsed two all-out federal assaults, thereby convincing Gen.Grant to lay siege to the seemingly impregnable Bluff City. After Gen. Joseph Johnston disobeyed President Davis's June command to relieve Vicksburg, General Pemberton had little choice but to ask Grant for terms. But when the Union leader made his famous "unconditional surrender" demand, Pemberton curtly replied that his men would continue fighting and "bury many more of your men before you enter Vicksburg." Grant quickly offered better terms and the Union flag once again flew above the courthouse cupola.

The National Military Park contains 1,330 acres, upon which are a national cemetery, sixteen hundred monuments and markers, twenty state memorials, nine Confederate forts, and miles of breastworks. It is listed in the National Register of Historic Places.

The Illinois Memorial, west elevation, is constructed of white Georgia marble in the style of the ancient Roman Parthenon. It stands sixty-two feet high and its circular exterior is etched with excerpts from speeches by President Lincoln and General Grant. Above the portico, supported by six, twenty-foot-tall, marble Doric columns, rests a bronze eagle symbolizing a reunited nation.

The Bobb House (McRaven)

1445 Harrison Street

Mississippi was still a part of Spanish West Florida in 1797 when the first part of McRaven was built as a Frontier-style, two-story, one-room-wide structure with an exterior staircase and gallery. An 1836 Federal-style addition by local sheriff Stephen Howard attached two more rooms and fronting galleries to the west wall, thereby altering the house's orientation toward the Mississippi River. Subsequent owner John Bobb wrought further changes in 1849, adding two more rooms onto the north end, thus reorienting the house to the north. The last addition was constructed in the Greek Revival style, as evidenced by the flying wing stairway, marble mantles, interior Grecian woodwork and plasterwork, and double-tiered gallery. However, these front galleries are supported with a celebrated Vicksburg idiom—Italianate pierced columns.

The house suffered cannon fire from both sides during the Battle of Vicksburg and served as a field hospital during the siege. John Bobb was killed in his garden by federal troops after the siege, and the home was later purchased by three sisters renowned for their reclusiveness. Because of careful restoration and preservation by the present owner, McRaven exists today practically unchanged since the Civil War and was nominated to the National Register of Historic Places in 1978.

McRaven, north elevation, is reputedly home to several supernatural residents, including former owner John Bobb, who was murdered in his garden by Yankee troops.

This frontier room was built in 1797. The original wall bricks were covered with plaster made of sugar, molasses, horsehair, and marble dust. The bed and hardwood flooring are also original, as are the tinwork candleholders and match, and candle keeper above the headboard.

The walls of the 1836 Howard bedroom are not wallpapered; they are decorated with period plaster. The canopied bed is fitted with mosquito netting and made of breakdown furniture, i.e. without nails and hinged for folding and laying flat for carriage transport.

McRaven's 1836 dining room has a Cazolla lamp above the original mahogany table, which burns cabbage and grape seed oil; a fourteen-hundred-piece set of rose medallion china, center; an original Audubon painting over the marble mantle; and a solid brass tea urn held aloft by Atlas.

This bedroom was built in 1849 by John Bobb and has a canopied Mallard bed with foot bars that raise up to support a mosquito net. A period-piece Mother of Pearl wedding fan graces the ladies' dresser, left, while a sitz tub rests atop the dresser, right. The low and armless Prelude chair allowed a lady to button her boots from side to side without bending over. The gasilier is of solid brass.

The front hall's flying wing staircase with walnut handrails and cypress steps. Beneath it is a mid-nineteenth century John Rogers sculpture of Romeo and Juliet, who watch over the Tussie-Mussie, or courting couch, shared in bygone days by a gentleman caller, a young lady of the house, and a matronly chaperon. The window treatments are of original velvet tapestry, and 1800s-era canes adorn a rose medallion umbrella stand. The wall-mounted mourning shadow box contains woven hair of the deceased.

Anchuca

1010 1st East Street

Vicksburg selectman J. W. Maulden built Anchuca as a one-story wood structure in 1830, but local merchant Victor Wilson's 1855 additions gave the home it's architectural significance. The two-story, gabled, low-pitched roof with dentiled cornice, the brick front section with inside-end chimneys, and a heavy entablature supported by four Doric columns, as well as the second-story pilastered entrance with side and transom lights are all indicative of the late Greek Revival style.

Situated in Vicksburg's oldest district, Anchuca was once owned by Joseph Davis, elder brother of Confederate Pres. Jefferson Davis, who once gave a rousing speech from the front, second floor gallery after Union troops burned the Davis plantation south of the city. The original slave quarters, built in 1847, are located behind the house, as is a lovely brick, New Orleans-style courtyard. Open to the public as part of the Vicksburg pilgrimage house tour, the six-thousand-square-foot mansion was named to the National Register of Historic Places in 1982.

Anchuca, south elevation, took its name from an Indian word meaning "happy home."

Anchuca's music room with an 1850 Broadwood piano; a cast-iron, coal-burning fireplace; and Berlin-work silk-thread screen; an 1810 painting above the mantle entitled, "Patterson Sisters"; a French Empire-style secretary and candelabra.

This Victorian bedroom features a canopied Mallard bed, an 1815 Federal-style bulls'-eye mirror, and two 1810 Old Paris vases resting atop a cast-iron mantle, which is itself covered by an 1820 French needlepoint screen.

Rolling Fork and Vicinity

While surveying land in this region in 1826 with government engineer and surveyor Stephen Howard, Thomas Y. Chaney bought a tract of land east of Deer Creek. Two years later, he named his plantation for the rolling water in a fork of Deer Creek near where it empties into the Sunflower River. After overcoming a Reconstruction-era race riot in 1875, the region's settlers got railroad service in 1883 and cultivated their first cotton crop in 1828 on an acre of land now occupied by the present county courthouse. A product of Petite Gulf seed, the first crop was sold in New Orleans in 1829 for fifty cents per pound.

Rolling Fork, located on Highway 61 between Vicksburg and Hollandale, is today a typical, quiet Delta hamlet, where the price of cotton is always a hot topic of conversation.

The Sharkey County Courthouse, west elevation, is located in the center of Rolling Fork's town square. It was built in 1902 in the Neo-Classical Revival style with fluted Ionic columns and triangular pediment.

Mount Helena

On old Highway 61, three miles northeast of Rolling Fork

In 1850, John Johnstone, an early settler of the Sharkey County region located a few miles east of the Mississippi River, established a twenty-five-hundred-acre plantation in the area, which he named after his daughter Helen. Her auspicious beginnings swiftly turned tragic when her fiancé, Henry Vick, a relative of Vicksburg's founder, Newitt Vick, was killed in a duel. Vick had promised Helen that he would never take a life in a duel, so when circumstances forced him onto the field of honor just days before their wedding date, he fired his shot in the air, only to receive a fatal bullet wound from his opponent. On the day planned for her wedding, Helen Johnstone, clad in her wedding gown, buried her betrothed on the grounds of Helena Plantation. Although she married Episcopal priest George Harris in 1896, she swore he would only have her hand and not her heart, which lay forever buried with Henry Vick.

Helen and George Harris built the Colonial Revival home, Mount Helena, in 1896, which, now as then, sits atop a ceremonial mound built by ancient Indians as a refuge from annual flooding. During the Great Flood of 1927, the Mississippi's waters covered ten feet of the mound. The home remains in the Johnstone/Harris family, and current owner Drick Rodgers began a sympathetic restoration in 1994.

Mount Helena, east elevation, features a widow's walk cupola, paired Ionic columns on all sides, fifteen fireplaces, a chapel, and a music room.

Mount Helena's defining Colonial Revival architectural features include upper-level balustrade; a second-story, center Palladian window; and fluted, paired Ionic columns supporting a portico with dentiled cornice.

Owner Drick Rodgers is restoring this stairway with turned balustrade and newel, classical columns, and a dramatic arch.

"Out in the distance, as far as the eye can see, the land is flat, dark and unbroken, sweeping away in a faint misty haze to the limits of the horizon. This is the great delta."   —*Willie Morris*

Yazoo City and Vicinity

Yazoo City is unique for being one of Mississippi's few planned communities. The area was initially chosen by Choctaw Chief Greenwood Leflore as part of his endowment from the 1926 Treaty of Doaks Stand, and he later sold his holdings to Jackson-area developers, who laid out a grid plan for a town on a bend of the nearby Yazoo River. The town was originally incorporated as Manchester in 1830, in honor ofthe Englishman who platted it. Nine years later it was renamed Yazoo City for the river on which it was situated, which was itself named for the sun-worshiping Indian tribe that once inhabited the region.

Part of Yazoo City is located on the Loess Bluffs, the hills that line the easternmost edge of the Mississippi Delta. The rest of the town is situated in the Delta flatlands and its residents call themselves Deltans (or as the purists maintain, Deltonians.) Along with the abundant natural pulchritude of the area, Yazooans have experienced their share of natural disasters, including several yellow fever epidemics, the floods of 1882 and 1927 (which covered the town's Delta portion to a depth of over twenty feet), and the worst fire in Mississippi history in 1904.

Yazoo also played a key role in the Civil War, as its naval yards produced the ironclad Arkansas, which single-handedly defeated the Union fleet in temporary relief of Vicksburg on July 15, 1862. The town also claims the youngest and oldest Confederate soldiers—Alexander Bailey, a thirteen-year-old cavalryman, and Jonathan Vancleave, a seventy-four-year-old infantryman. Other notable Yazooans include U.S. Sen. John Sharpe Williams (1834-1931), author Willie Morris (1934-2000), and former U.S. Secretary of Agriculture, Mike Espy (1953-).

Delta swamp or "hardwood brake."

No Mistake Plantation

5602 Highway 3, south of Yazoo City

When Andrew Jackson rode through the region that would later become Yazoo City, one of his men, David Smith, took note of the countryside's extravagant natural beauty. Years later, his five sons settled in the region, among them John William Smith, who had difficulty choosing among several attractive locations. When he asked his brothers for advice, one of them replied that Smith's favored site, surrounded by rolling countryside and willow trees, was "no mistake." Smith promptly purchased those twelve thousand acres at $1.25 per acre and established No Mistake Plantation in 1833. This house was constructed ten years later.

The sloping dormered roof and eight Ionic columns on a broad veranda with dentiled cornice are indicative of No Mistake's Greek Revival style, although much of the interior is decorated in the late Victorian style. Situated among lovely gardens on a seven-acre complex, the one-and-a-half-story cottage remained in the Smith family for over six generations until recently purchased by the present owners, Cindy and Jerry Graves.

No Mistake Plantation, north elevation, with hybrid day lilies.

No Mistake's music room, formerly a Victorian parlor, is still partly decorated in the Victorian rococo style, including the table and chairs with gracefully-curved Cabriole legs. A stained-glass transom highlights a Victorian-style window.

Gardens line No Mistake's driveways.

41

The P-Line House
10605 Eagle Bend Road

Built in 1840 by architect James Galtney, this Greek Revival farmhouse was acquired by James Knox Dent in 1860 and has been in the Dent/Kinkead family for seven succeeding generations. In the 1860s, James Dent was a steamboat captain on the Parisot Line, transporting cotton and passengers down the Yazoo River to Vicksburg. He married Annie Kinkead, the daughter of a plantation owner, and together they formed a partnership with Sherman Parisot, the owner of the largest steamboat line in the region. The Dent home became known as the P-Line House because it served as the line's headquarters north of Vicksburg. Their daughter, Annie Kinkead Dent, led the women's suffrage movement in turn-of-the-century Mississippi.

The P-Line House is a true four-room, center-hall home, and its authentic dogtrot hallway opens in the front onto the Yazoo River, a mere one hundred feet away, affording a unique bird's-eye view of passing ships. A full-front gallery supported by six, square Doric columns overlooks not only the Yazoo River, but also the original Corps of Engineers' 1920s levee, as well as a towering, one-hundred-fifty-year-old pecan tree. The back door opens onto twenty-two hundred acres of family-owned cotton farming land.

The P-Line House, northwest elevation.

The P-Line house's center hallway opens onto a front gallery through double leaf doors with horizontal transom and sidelights. The nearby secretary, left, and hall tree, right, are original. The hardwood hall flooring is pine.

The Heart of the Mississippi Delta

". . . [T]he rich black land, imponderable and vast,
fecund up to the very doorsteps of the black men
who worked it and the white men who owned it . . ."
—William Faulkner

LAKE WASHINGTON VICINITY

Eighteen miles south of Greenville, just west of Highway 1, lies Lake
Washington, formed from two separate bends of the Mississippi River before
that stream changed course and moved further to the west. Situated on the
lake are three tiny communities established in the late 1820s and early
1830s—Erwin, Foote, and Glen Allen.

Choctaw Indian guides led Indian agent Robert Ward to a place so beautiful that, in 1825, he purchased two thousand acres from the Choctaws for $50
in gold pieces and a keg of whiskey. He later deeded the land to his eighteen-
year-old son, Kentucky planter Junius Ward, who came down river on flatboats in 1830 and built the Erwin House at the head of Lake Washington.
Erwin, the village that grew around Ward's house, eventually reached a population of two hundred, and boasted its own railroad station, post office, and
cotton gin. A mile north of Erwin is the old community of Foote, which arose
on land originally purchased from the government by Junius Ward. It was later
owned by Henry and Elizabeth Johnson, who, in 1838, owned 2,180 acres of
land and 103 slaves. In 1855, Johnson sold part of his then four thousand
acres to his daughter Margaret for $100,000. It was on that land that she built
the imposing antebellum mansion, Mount Holly, a stone's throw from beautiful Lake Washington.

Several miles to the south of Foote is land originally purchased by Fredrick
G. Turnbull for use as a cotton plantation. He sold his holdings there to Wade
and Christopher Hampton in the late 1840s. Scotsman S. M. Spencer purchased the plantation in the early 1860s and named it Glen Allen. The hamlet which grew up around it took the plantation's name, as was the custom of
the period. P. L. Mann, a wealthy planter and politician, built Linden there on
the shores of Lake Washington in 1914.

Desirous of having their own church, the Hamptons, Turnbulls, and other
early settlers built the Delta's first Episcopal church at Glen Allen in 1855.
Today, the magnificent ruins of St. John's Protestant Episcopal Church is a
haunting reminder of the grandeur that once graced these three ancient Lake
Washington communities.

Ruins of St. John's Episcopal Church
Greenfield Cemetery, northeast of Glen Allen
on Lake Washington

St. John's was the first Episcopal church in the Delta, built in 1856 in English-Gothic design by slave labor. Jesse Crowell, a slave belonging to the church warden, Robert J. Turnbull, supervised the construction, using lumber from the nearby forest and bricks prepared on the site. A skilled craftsman, Crowell carved the wood for the pews, doors, window casings, chancel rail, and pulpit. After the church's completion, Crowell served as St. John's sexton until his death.

Bishop William Mercer Green, Sr., who consecrated the church on April 5, 1857, described it in his journal as "one of the most finished and tasty structures . . . in the whole Southwest." The building featured plaster-coated red brick, flying buttresses, and stained-glass windows, from which lead was extracted and melted to make Confederate mini-balls during the Civil War. Wade Hampton, scion of the South Carolina plantation empire Hamptons, served as one of the church's original vestrymen and achieved subsequent fame as a Confederate general and as governor of South Carolina.

During the hard times after the Civil War, the church fell into disrepair, but extensive turn-of-the-century renovation efforts were dashed by a 1907 tornado that tore off the roof and demolished most of the building. All that remains are a few cornerstones, wall sections, and a portion of the short belfry.

Ruins of St. John's Episcopal Church, southwest elevation.

Junius B. Ward House (Erwin House)

North end of Lake Washington near Highway 1 in Erwin

The Erwin House, built on the site of an earlier log cabin, is the oldest extant structure in Washington County. Built in 1830 by Kentucky planter Junius B. Ward, the one-and-a-half-story house is an excellent example of Mississippi vernacular architecture of the period. It is constructed of half-notched logs covered by white clapboard, stands on a brick pier foundation, and features buttressed chimneys on gabled ends. It was built in the traditional single-pile formula of a central hall, flanked by a parlor and dining room on either side. The rear loggia was enclosed in 1910 and one of the rear cabinets extended in 1925.

Junius Ward's daughter, Matilda, purchased the property in 1877 and later married Johnson Erwin of nearby Mount Holly. Their son, Victor Erwin, married Margaret Preston McNeilly, the daughter of Confederate veteran J. S. McNeilly, a prominent newspaper publisher and one of the framers of Mississippi's current 1890 constitution. Their daughter Margaret Erwin Shutt and her husband William acquired the Erwin House in 1940 and restored it in such a manner as to warrant its listing on the National Register of Historic Places in 1975.

The Junius B. Ward House (Erwin), west elevation, overlooks what is generally considered to be the most picturesque view of nearby Lake Washington.

Mount Holly

Between Highway 1 and Lake Washington in Foote

A two-story, red brick, Italianate mansion of thirty-two rooms, Mount Holly was built in 1855 by Dr. Charles Wilkins Dudley for his wife, Margaret Johnson Erwin Dudley. The round arches, bay windows, brackets, Palladian-style main entrance archway, and wrought-iron balcony railings are features common to the nineteenth century Italian villa style. Interior features include a rosewood staircase with trumpet balusters and fourteen-foot-high ceilings bordered by decorative friezes and centered with plaster medallions and brass chandeliers. It was likely designed by architect Samuel Sloan, who designed Longwood in Natchez, although the mansion bears a striking resemblance to another designed by architect Calvert Vaux.

In the 1880s, the mansion was acquired by William H. Foote, a former Confederate officer and prominent attorney who also owned three other Delta plantations. His son Huger Lee Foote, a merchant, planter, and state senator, inherited the house. His grandson, noted author and Civil War historian Shelby Foote, used Huger Lee Foote as inspiration for the protagonist of his 1949 novel, *Tournament.*

Mount Holly, west elevation, was named to the National Register of Historic Places in 1973.

Linden

Between Highway 1 and Lake Washington at Glen Allen

Linden was built in 1914 by architects E. N. Alger of West Virginia and H. H. Davis of Vicksburg for planter and prominent turn-of-the-century political figure P. L. Mann. It is situated on property owned in the late 1850s by Confederate Gen. Wade Hampton, but Mann razed the Hampton house in order to build Linden. It remained in continuous ownership by one family until recently purchased by the current owner, Nancy Bridges, who has converted it into a bed and breakfast inn called Linden-on-the-Lake.

The two-and-a-half-story, twenty-room, brick mansion was constructed in the Neo-Classical style with a front-gabled roof and giant, pedimented, two-story portico supported by four, massive, fluted, Ionic columns. The northerly porch extends to form a porte-cochere, and the double front door is framed by fanlight transom and sidelights. The interior has a wide center hall flanked by parlors on either side and retains the original brass fixtures in three bathrooms, while the paneled wall of the formal rooms all retain their original silk covering.

Linden, west elevation, was listed on the National Register of Historic Places in 1982.

"With us, when you speak of `the river,' though there are many, you mean the great river, the shifting unappeasable god of the country, feared and loved, the Mississippi."   —*William Alexander Percy*

GREENVILLE

Now the county seat of Washington County and the most populous (approximately 50,000) of all Delta towns, Greenville had to overcome extraordinary difficulties that would have finished many other river towns. Its history begins in 1828, when Col. William W. Blanton established Blantonia Plantation on the banks of the Mississippi River. Efforts to found a town on two previous sites in the area were blunted first by river-induced erosion and later in 1863 by the shelling of federal gunboats, which set the budding town ablaze. Finally in 1870, on land donated by Blanton's widow, the then Mrs. Harriet B. Theobold, Greenville was incorporated at its present location.

But the worst was yet to come. An 1878 yellow fever epidemic wiped out a third of Greenville's population, while block after block of the town continued to crumble into the river. Regular floods proved a major problem, culminating in the Great Flood of 1927, which left Greenville under water for seventy days and cost the Delta five hundred lives and $200 million. Greenvillians rose above these difficulties by installing a worthy levee system in the late 1920s, which lead to the establishment of enormous cotton trade wealth. They also forged the Delta's twentieth century intellectual and literary renaissance, with poet William Alexander Percy, author Bern Keating, novelists Walker Percy, Shelby Foote, and Ellen Douglas, and Pulitzer Prize-winning journalist Hodding Carter, Jr., at the center of a literary explosion unexcelled by that of any other similarly-sized town in America.

Washington Avenue, home to several antebellum cottages, was included in the National Register's Historic District in 1984.

The First National Bank Building
302 Main Street

A block from Greenville's historic Cotton Row is the site of the first feder-ally-chartered bank in Washington County. This is the former First National Bank, which was founded in 1903 by James E. Negus, Jr., a Civil War Union Officer who had relocated in Greenville during Reconstruction in 1870. Negus himself traveled to Italy to select the marble and stained glass for the bank's skylight. Erected at a cost of $50,000, the one-story, brick building was fashioned in the Neo-Classical Revival style, with a recessed, three-bay por-tico of four, pedestaled, Roman Ionic columns, a full entablature, and richly-detailed triangular pediment. The columns and steps are made of grey Tennessee marble, as are the carved marble quoins and coping.

With a starting capital of $100,000 in 1903, the bank prospered through-out the Great Depression when fourteen of Mississippi's seventeen nationally-chartered banks failed. Notable members of the bank's board of directors include U.S. Sen. Leroy Percy and his son, author William Alexander Percy. It is now a municipal courts building.

The First National Bank Building, southwest elevation, was named to the National Register of Historic Places in 1978.

St. Joseph Roman Catholic Church
412 Main Street

Greenville-area Catholics began raising money for a church shortly after the town was incorporated, and in 1874 they purchased land for that purpose from Mrs. Harriet Theobold, upon whose former plantation land Greenville was built. At the time, Bishop William Henry Elder noted that funds for the proposed church were raised, "by the liberality of citizens, Catholic and non-Catholic, and by the never failing generosity, of the Irish laborers on the railroads and levees."

The present building replaced the first church in 1907. St. Joseph was designed and financed by Father P. J. Korsternbrock, a Dutch nobleman, who renounced his nobility, moved to Greenville, and served as parish priest for thirty-three years. The Dutch Gothic Revival church is a replica of a Haarland, Netherlands cathedral, and its stained-glass windows hail from the Munich Studios of Emil Frei.

St. Joseph Roman Catholic Church, southwest elevation.

Hebrew Union Temple
504 Main Street

Greenville's Jewish community dates back to 1867 and includes the city's first elected mayor, Leopold Wilzinski. Mississippi's largest Jewish congregation was originally organized in Greenville in 1880 and served by Dr. Joseph Bogen, their first settled rabbi, from 1881-1901. The present temple was erected in 1906 at a cost of $30,000 and dedicated on October 27. The Ark and one of the three Torahs have been in use since 1882.

This brick and stone structure is of the Neo-Classical Revival style, with a pedimented portico supported by two sets of paired Ionic columns, and features ornamental stained-glass memorial windows. It suffered damage from flooding in 1927 and 1939, requiring repair and redecoration both years.

Hebrew Union Temple, southwest elevation. While building their new sanctuary in the early 1900s, the Greenville First Methodists were guest occupants of the temple on Sundays.

Griffin-Spragins House (Refuge Plantation)
Off Highway 82 just before the Mississippi River Bridge

This one-story, framed, enlarged cottage structure was built in 1830 in the early Greek Revival style by South Carolina émigré Francis Griffin. After serving in the War of 1812, Griffin settled in Warren County where he established Magnolia plantation and after his first wife died, married her cousin, Leonora Scarlett. After meeting financial reverses, the Griffins purchased land in Washington County and built a home he named Griffin's Refuge, for his escape from early misfortune. Griffin later served in the state legislature and as a county judge, and worked the plantation with his son, John.

The younger Griffin, who is credited with inventing both the first cotton picker and rolling skates, helped build Refuge into a successful enterprise. On two separate occasions, the Griffins were forced to escape the encroaching Mississippi River by jacking up their home and rolling it on logs to higher land. Like many local planters, they lost much of their fortune during the Civil War and were forced to sell Refuge Plantation in the late 1870s.

A subsequent owner, Edmund Richardson, utilized questionable practices, including the use of convict labor, that helped make him so successful that he was dubbed "the largest cotton planter in the world—except, perhaps, the Khedive of Egypt." By 1880, his company, Richardson and May, had become the largest cotton factorage in the United States.

Refuge Plantation was named to the National Register of Historic Places in 1984. 53

Belmont

Intersection of Highways 1 and 438 at Wayside

Belmont is located a few miles south of Greenville on land first owned in 1832 by Mississippi Gov. Alexander G. McNutt (1838-1843) and later purchased in 1853 by Kentuckian Samuel Worthington, one of the first white settlers (1820) in Washington County. Wealthy planter William Worthington bought the land from his brother in 1855 and constructed Belmont two years later as his private residence. It would survive as one of the few antebellum homes in the region not burned by rampaging Union soldiers.

The two-story, red brick building was built in the high Federal style, with centered gable and five ranks of symmetrically-aligned windows, although its stacked porches are linked by classical columns with Italianate detailing. It is further distinguished by fourteen-foot-high ceilings, nine fireplaces, and a central hall flanked by two twenty-by-twenty parlors.

Belmont is the private residence of Mr. and Mrs. Fernando J. Cuquet, Jr., who acquired it in 1993 and have made extensive renovations. Mr. Cuquet, a colorful character, is a former New Orleans attorney and banker who developed the Delta's first casinos in Tunica and Greenville. He also served as a WWII American spy and later helped the F.B.I. solve a notorious white slavery case.

Belmont, west elevation, was named to the National Register of Historic Places in 1984.

Architectural details of one of Belmont's downstairs double-parlors include fourteen-foot ceilings, floor-length window casings with croissettes, elaborate plaster ceilings, and a cast-iron mantlepiece with a molded fireplace arch opening beneath a cartouche, and spandrels and a rounded shelf.

Belmont's stair hall is part of a central hall floor plan with two twenty-by-twenty rooms on each side. The elaborate ceiling plasterwork consists of cornice, borderwork, paterae, and medallions that feature a melange of flowers, foliage, and fruit. A stairway of twenty risers runs straight from the prominent newel to the second floor. The broad handrail is carried by a balustrade of turned balusters, two to a thread, which extends around the second-floor hallway.

"The proud white people thought they were lords of creation, and no 'damyankees' could make them change their minds or their ways. Pleasure was the chief concern of their lives, and they sought it and had it, just as their parents had done in the good old days."
—*Mrs. Upton Sinclair*

GREENWOOD

Due east of Greenville on Highway 82 is Greenwood, Mississippi's most significant cotton market and the largest inland, long staple cotton market in the world. Like much of the interior Delta, the area that is now Greenwood was once little more than alligator, bear, snake, and cougar-infested swamps and hardwood forests until the mid-nineteenth century. The 1830 Treaty of Dancing Rabbit Creek opened the land up to white settlement, and in 1834 John Williams came up the Yazoo River and began clearing 162 acres near the junction of the Tallahatchie and Yalobusha Rivers, where they meet to form the Yazoo.

This area became known as Williams Landing, and despite Choctaw chief, U.S. senator, and prominent planter Greenwood Leflore's efforts to put it out of business, it flourished as a shipping point for local farmers' cotton. Incorporated in 1844, Greenwood produced many of the wealthiest planters in the state, who took full advantage of the fifteen- to sixty-five-foot-deep top-soil on the most fertile land in the United States.

In 1862 a significant Civil War battle was waged at Greenwood, where Confederates scuttled the captured Union gunboat, the *Star of the West*, in the Tallahatchie River near Fort Pemberton, and sprung an ambush that halted Grant's backdoor approach to Vicksburg. Despite the victory, the war and Reconstruction brought hard times to Greenwood and the Delta.

After being named county seat of Leflore in 1871 and receiving railroad lines in the 1880s, the town figured prominently in the postbellum cotton boom of the 1890s. Local factors loaned farmers money for spring planting, took a lien on their land, provided storage and shipping after picking, and negotiated the best available deals for planters in Memphis and New Orleans. Using this system, Greenwood not only cornered much of the Mississippi market, but also became one of the world's most successful cotton-producing towns.

Historic Cotton Row District
100 block of Front Street

Fifty-seven buildings located a mere stone's throw from the Yazoo River in downtown Greenwood comprise the Historic Cotton Row District. The original buildings in this area were made of wood as late as 1879, but recurring fires forced the cotton factors to rebuild their structures out of brick. Even the district's streets were bricked between 1914 and 1917, although only the ones on Main and Market Streets have escaped being covered over with asphalt in recent years.

Several law offices and a bank are located in the district, but most of its buildings have always been owned by cotton factors. This changed abruptly in 1997 when Viking Range Corporation purchased and renovated several buildings in the 100 block of Front Street, overlooking the Yazoo. Taking advantage of federal preservation tax incentives, Viking made a sympathetic restoration of an 1895 building on Cotton Row, which now serves as its headquarters. Viking has continued its preservation and restoration of other Cotton Row buildings, adding to the architectural integrity of a district that was listed on the National Register of Historic Places in 1980.

This section of Historic Cotton Row, north elevation, is now home to Viking Range Corporation.

Lusco's

722 Carrollton Avenue

Greenwood's oldest and most celebrated restaurant, Lusco's was a grocery with a very small menu when it opened in 1923 in this one-story, flat-roofed, two-bay, red brick building. During Prohibition, Charles Lusco added privately-partitioned booths in the rear for revelry, dining, and the sampling of home-made beer and "bathtub Gin." Patrons were escorted from the main room to linen, table cloth-covered tables in small, curtained rooms, where they could enjoy Prohibition's illicit delights in perfect anonymity.

The building was expanded in the early 1940s to take in an adjoining structure that had formerly been a drugstore. Since Lusco's is located next door to the New Zion Missionary Baptist Church (b. 1920), only beer is available, although wine and liquor may be brought in, or "brown bagged," in the local vernacular. Untouched by modern decoration or alteration, Lusco's offers a unique atmosphere in which to enjoy pompano and steaks. The restaurant is now in its fifth generation of ownership in one family.

Lusco's Restaurant, north elevation.

Leflore County Courthouse
310 W. Market Street

A key element of the Historic Cotton Row District is the Leflore County Courthouse, a Beaux-Arts Neo-Classical Revival building erected in 1906. Designed by architect Reuben Harrison Hunt, this two-story, rectangular-block building features a center, full-height, tetrastyle pedimental entrance portico supported by four, massive Ionic columns, and a mansard roof with a central, four-faced clock tower and dome.

The Neo-Classical Revival style was originally designed to emphasize America's bright economic horizons with massive, pedimented porticos supported by equally-robust classical columns, as opposed to the smaller projections and varied roof lines of the Victorian era. The new style proved an ideal choice for this courthouse, which was built during the town's meteoric rise to prominence as Mississippi's leading cotton market.

The Leflore County Courthouse, south elevation, stands on former Choctaw lands once used for tribal trial and execution.

River Oaks
601 River Road

Located in the River Road and Western Downtown Residential Historic District, surrounded by huge oaks, and overlooking the Yazoo River, River Oaks was built in 1905 at a cost of $75,000. This two-story, stuccoed-and-scored-frame mansion has a giant-order single-bay portico supported by eight, fluted Ionic columns, paired columns, long runs of balustrade, and the sixty-four-foot-long full-front porch with superimposed two-story portico which identify its Colonial Revival style. Windows are filled with original one-over-one double-hung sash and are uniformly arranged in single units.

River Oaks, north elevation, was briefly used as a funeral parlor, but it was restored in 1952 by Carl Kelly and is now the private residence of Mr. and Mrs. Jack Hodges.

Originally owned by a doctor, River Oaks was later purchased by a wealthy planter who is said to have entertained there in high Delta style. After ensconcing the orchestra on several of the seven curved, oak steps of the first flight stairway, he opened the huge, quarter-sawed, sliding pocket doors between the library, living room, and dining room and converted the entire area into a dance floor. Note the paired, fluted, oak columns with Corinthian capitals supporting the graceful archway.

Bridgewater Inn
501 River Road

Stephens Collins Foster was so impressed with the lovely view of the Yazoo River afforded by Greenwood's River Road that he wrote a song that began, "Way down upon the Yazoo River, far, far away." But his publisher didn't care for the name "Yazoo," and insisted that Foster substitute the name Sewanee, a river that Foster never saw in his life.

That same breathtaking vista may be enjoyed today from the second-floor porch of the Bridgewater Inn, a Neo-Classical Revival mansion erected in 1915. The fluted, Corinthian columns, cast-iron railings, square-head windows, and glazed French doors are indicative of the turn-of-the-century Neo-Classical style, reflecting back to an era of cotton-forged affluence.

Bridgewater Inn's second floor porch, north elevation, with view of Keesler Bridge and the Yazoo River.

Bridgewater Inn, north elevation, now operated as a romantic bed and breakfast, was built in the Neo-Classical Revival style with tetrastyle fluted Corinthian columns supporting a full-width, double-tiered porch, square-headed windows, and a cast-iron railing. The center-bay frontispiece entrance features a single-leaf door with stained-glass panels set beneath a fanlight transom. The second-story entrance is a double-leaf door with leaded-glass upper panel set beneath a multi-light transom.

Revelee (The Gwin House)
810 Grand Boulevard

Capt. Samuel L. Gwin built this house in 1915 as part of a planned residential neighborhood to be centered along an oak-lined boulevard. He began by purchasing land that had once been part of U.S. Senator J. Z. George's plantation. Gwin next transformed those fields into ten-acre lots, with side streets intersecting the boulevard every four hundred feet.

Gwin's wife, Sally, began planting trees along the boulevard in 1916. After locating prospects by horseback on the Tallahatchie's banks, Mrs. Gwin had her crew foreman uproot them, load them onto wagons filled with water buckets, and plant them along the roadway.

This 10,000-square-foot mansion was designed by architect Frank R. McGeoy in the Colonial Revival style, as evidenced by its side porch, hipped roof and paired windows with double-hung sash. The Neo-Classical pedimented entry portico with Ionic columns is a later addition. It is now the private residence of local attorney Lee Abraham, Jr., who has performed much-needed restoration.

Revelee, west elevation, was built on the highest point in North Greenwood. The rear English Garden, south-elevation sleeping porch, and rear dancing patio are all original, as is an interior, three-story laundry chute.

Sally Humphreys Gwin often entertained up to five hundred revelers at parties in this mansion. She served governors and ex-confederate generals in this dining room, and the mirror is a twin to another currently hanging in the Mississippi Governor's Mansion in Jackson. The room opens onto an original sun porch.

This second-story sleeping porch features an 1830s poster bed and a trough between the pine floor and outer wall that was installed to drain off water blown through the porch's mosquito screens.

Carter House
President and Grand Boulevard

This Colonial Revival, raised cottage, built in 1907 by circuit clerk C. W. Crocket, was originally erected in a location that would have placed it squarely in the middle of Capt. Samuel L. Gwin's proposed Grand Boulevard. But Crockett agreed to move his house a few hundred feet to the northeast, where it could face the soon-to-be-completed boulevard. This was accomplished by rolling huge logs under the foundation, hooking mule teams to the frame, and rolling it to its new destination. But the workers mistakenly left the house facing a side street, so today it is the only Boulevard home that doesn't face the Boulevard.

It is now the private residence of Dr. and Mrs. Michael Carter, who acquired it in 1979, and is the oldest house in the Grand Boulevard Historical District. The single-dormered, hipped roof, turned Ionic columns supporting a full-length porch, clapboard siding, and twelve-foot ceilings are indicative of the house's architectural style.

Carter House, south elevation.

This authentic dogtrot hallway has a twelve-foot-high ceiling, working transoms above the doors, oak flooring, and a Victorian musical motif with batten molding made of figured red gum.

Heavy pocket doors separate the west parlor and dining room. The west-elevation, dining-room bay window faces Grand Boulevard.

Provine House
319 Grand Boulevard

One of Greenwood's best examples of the Neo-Classical Revival style, the Provine House was built for cotton factor Braxton Bragg Provine in 1910 by Tennessee architect H. C. White at a cost of $6,000. In addition to owning a cotton company, Provine also had part ownership of the Bank of Greenwood and a Memphis compress and storage company, and also served as President of the Greenwood Cotton Exchange and as city commissioner.

With its impressive portico, full entablature, and fluted, Ionic columns, the Provine House attracted Hollywood's attention in 1968 when *The Reivers*, based upon William Faulkner's novel, was filmed in Greenwood. Both Grand Boulevard and the Provine House figured prominently in the film, which starred Steve McQueen. It is now the private residence of Dr. and Mrs. Samuel H. Lambdin, who repaired the damage incurred when the Tallahatchie over-ran its banks in 1932 and flooded the Boulevard with several feet of water.

The Provine House, east elevation, was listed on the National Register of Historic Places in 1980.

The elaborately-treated dining room features oak paneling and exposed oak beams. The wide doorways between the dining room and reception hall have a pair of oversized pocket doors. A set of Mint Julep cups add to the old South ambiance.

The Provine House's center-bay entrance doorway is fronted by a smaller, flat-roof portico supported by fluted Ionic columns. It features a single-leaf door set within oversized, leaded-glass side-lights beneath a leaded-glass, full-width transom.

Grand Boulevard Historic District
Grand Boulevard

The largest and most architecturally significant residential neighborhood in Greenwood, the Grand Boulevard Historic District is perhaps the best surviving evidence of the town's affluence after it became the center of Mississippi's post-bellum cotton kingdom. Shaded by towering pin oaks, this wide boulevard runs a mile between the Yazoo and Tallahatchie Rivers and is bordered by beautiful homes of various architectural styles, including Spanish Eclectic, Neo-Classical Revival, Tudor, Prairie, and Colonial Revival. Many of the cross streets display good examples of Bungalow, Spanish Eclectic, and Tudor cottages.

Capt. Samuel L. Gwin consummated his Grand Boulevard scheme within a scant few years, as the 1919 letter of a Greenwood tourist notes: "That old jungle on the other side [of the Yazoo River] bids fair to become one of the prettiest residence sections in the country, with a magnificent boulevard . . . lined on either side with elegant homes and spacious grounds. One party [Will Humphreys], the senior member of a local cotton firm that buys and sells over one-tenth of the entire cotton crop of Mississippi . . . is building a $100,000 residence on this Boulevard, near the Tallahatchie."

That home would later come to be known as Rosemary, and it would be one of many lovely houses in the Grand Boulevard Historic District, which was listed on the National Register of Historic Places in 1986.

Grand Boulevard Historic District, north elevation.

Bellashon

805 Poplar

This two-story, 10,000-square-foot, Neo-Classical Revival mansion with a full-width gallery and fluted Corinthian columns was built by Charles and Aleeta Billups Saunders in 1925. Aleeta's father was Rowell Billups, the founder of Billups Oil Company, and she named Bellashon after a 1648 Virginia mansion erected by her father's forebear, George Billups. It is now the private residence of Rowell Billup's grandson, Rowell Billups Saunders.

Built to withstand almost any contingency, Bellashon has lead, fire walls and was constructed on top of twelve four-by-four concrete piers topped by a series of twelve-inch-wide beams that run the length of the house, insuring it against earthquake. The mansion's indoor temperature is regulated via a rear elevation pump house where fans force air through a large radiator which can either heat or cool the air before it is pumped through a series of pipes and vents throughout Bellashon. Additional ventilation is readily available by virtue of thirteen double-leaf, glazed, French doors on the front elevation.

Bellashon, east elevation, has a hipped roof porte-cochere on the north elevation.

Bellashon's library was crafted of hand-carved California beechwood, a gift from the Seeburg family, renowned for its jukebox company.

The curving staircase was handmade of large blocks of walnut, not bent but "cut to the curve." The flooring is of Italian marble. The hallway is decorated with Louis XIV antiques.

Bellashon's living room is decorated with a Saborney rug, Louis XIV chairs and mirror, and a two-hundred-year-old Bhoem cabinet with red tortoise inlay. The silk drapes are a duplicate of those originally made for the Nixon White House. Aleeta Billups crafted the chandelier of New Orleans wrought iron and candle sconces.

This ladies makeup boudoir was once given as a wedding gift to Mary Therese by the archduke of Austria, the last gift given by the Holy Roman Emperor. It was later owned by the infamous Mata Hari before being given to Rowell Billups in thanks for saving European Jews from the Nazis by bringing them to America to work for Billups Petroleum Company. The porcelain pictures depict classic romantic scenes.

Bledsoe House
1012 Grand Boulevard

This stuccoed-brick residence was built in 1925 by planter Oscar Bledsoe, founder and president of Staplcotn, Greenwood's most significant cotton-marketing business since its inception in 1920. Local legend has it that, while riding a train to Memphis, Bledsoe overheard a Memphis cotton merchant bragging about making his entire year's salary off a deal he had made with Greenwood-area planters. Bledsoe's response was to join up with other Delta planters such as Sen. Leroy Percy and William M. Gerard to found a cooperative marketing association named Staplcotn, which allowed them to market their yield on better terms of their own choosing. Within four years, Staplcotn had marketed over $80 million worth of Delta cotton.

Modeled after its architect George Mahon's Memphis residence, this building represents an American adaptation of the Mediterranean style. Although the red, barrel-tiled roof, heavy wooden front door, multi-arched chimney cover, and stuccoed-tile walls are of the Spanish Eclectic style, the eave overhang, pillared veranda, tall round-headed windows, and entrance portico with Ionic columns and dolphin-decorated capitals are aspects of the Italian Renaissance or villa style.

Bledsoe House, southwest elevation.

The Bledsoe House living room with French Empire mirror and ceiling plasterwork with dolphin medallions. The room opens onto a south elevation solarium.

The Bledsoe House entrance doorway is defined by a single-bay shallow portico with full entablature supported by Ionic columns and adorned with bas-relief garlands. Elaborate plasterwork surrounds the heavy wooden Spanish door, and the column capitals are decorated with a dolphin design.

The dining room flooring is of grey Georgia marble. Wrought iron doors open onto a period piece dining table, and reflected in the French Empire mirror is a five-hundred-year-old oriental statue.

75

Rosemary

1440 Grand Boulevard

Built in 1920 for prominent cotton merchant Will Humphreys by Memphis architect George Mahon, this is one of Greenwood's most significant examples of Tudor-style architecture. Originally named "Eleven Acres," this two-story, stuccoed, private residence is now situated on 7.75 acres overlooking the Tallahatchie River.

In 1933, the house was purchased by cotton merchant William Garrard. Frequent guests in the Garrard home included neighbor and partner Oscar Bledsoe, who founded Staplcotn in 1920, and Greenville poet and author William Alexander Percy, son of Staplcotn cofounder Sen. Leroy Percy. Social events often led to skeet shooting over the river from the second-floor skeet porch. The Garrards renamed the house Rosemary, for the Shakespearean line, "Rosemary for remembrance." It is now the private residence of Charlotte Saunders Ray, the granddaughter of oil magnate Rowell Billups, and sister of Bellashon's owner, Rowell Saunders.

Rosemary, west elevation, was listed on the National Register of Historic Places in 1985.

Rosemary's three sun-parlor skylights illuminate an original fireplace with unique railroad tie irons. The painting above the mantle is by Mississippi artist Bill Dunlap. The table, right, is of Turkish and Italian marble.

Rosemary's master bathroom with two skylights, a tile floor, a marble hot tub, and paintings by popular local artists.

Jones House
17610 County Road 559, just north of Schlater

The hamlet of Schlater, pronounced "slaughter," is located fifteen miles northwest of Greenwood on Highway 49. It was originally named "Maryland," for planter Randall Blewitt's fiancée, but her faithlessness during his Confederate service at the Battle of Manassas prompted the severely-wounded Blewitt to change his will and leave his 889 acres to a nephew, Randall Blewitt Schlater, for whom the town was renamed in 1911.

Four Jones brothers comprised one of Schlater's most prominent early families, and one them, a planter named Ed, built a beautiful, pink, stuccoed house known locally as the "Pink Palace," which later burned. His brother, David Smith Jones, built the first house on this property in 1912. It burned in 1929, and his widow, Mabel, rebuilt a one-story structure in its place. Her son added a second floor in 1954. This Neo-Classical Revival building with four, square Doric columns is now the residence of Mr. and Mrs. James P. Cole and has remained in the same family for four generations.

Jones House, north elevation.

Jones House parlor, leading into the dining room. The mirror on the far wall is a Renaissance Revival piece designed by the Herta Brothers. It and six other Herta Brothers mirrors were purchased at an auction in the 1950s from the California home of millionaire and philanthropist Darius Ogden Mills.

Large Herta Brothers mirror reflects two companion pieces, one with a center hall tree, and another against the front wall in the adjoining library.

79

Rosedale's Grace Episcopal Church, built in 1879, is the oldest church in Bolivar County. It is of a vernacular Carpenter Gothic style with weatherboard siding, a steeply-pitched roof, and a gabled entry porch supported by two Tuscan columns. It was named to the National Register of Historic Places in 1981.

> "I also lived in the low cotton country where moon-
> light hovered over ripe haystacks, or stumps or trees,
> and croppers' rotting shacks, with famine, terror,
> flood and plague near by. . . ."
> —*Margaret Walker Alexander*

CLEVELAND AND VICINITY

Cleveland, twenty miles to the west of Rosedale on Highway 8, is the county seat of Bolivar. It was once known as Simms, after its founder B. C. Simms, but he later renamed it in honor of Pres. Grover C. Cleveland. The establishment of what is now Delta State University in 1924 assured Cleveland's status as one of the Delta's leading communities well into the twenty-first century

In 1838, Virginia planter Col. Lafayette Jones left his Charlottesville plantation to form a landing on the Mississippi River one mile north of what is now Rosedale, in Bolivar County. Located halfway between Greenville and Clarksdale, Rosedale is called the "City of Roses," for its abundant riverside rose gardens.

Mound Bayou, fifteen miles north of Cleveland on Highway 61, had its beginnings in another settlement, namely on Jefferson Davis's Hurricane Plantation, located twenty miles south of Vicksburg. A former U.S. Secretary of War and future President of the Confederate States of America, Jefferson and his brother Joseph had developed the idea that free, economically-independent blacks living in their own isolated settlements was a viable alternative to the vicissitudes of slavery.

In 1865, two of their former slaves, Isaiah T. Montgomery and his cousin Benjamin Green, succeeded in establishing the very enterprise imagined by the Davises. Years later, they moved to a Delta site where an ancient Indian Mound bridged two primordial bayous.

Montgomery named the new settlement Mound Bayou in 1887, and he and his companions immediately began reclaiming it from the forests and swamps. All of them had one goal in mind—to live free from any constraints upon their liberty, equality, and pursuit of economic prosperity and self-government. By the turn of the century, the Mound Bayou experiment had proved an unqualified success. The settlers had opened a bank by 1904, constructed their own oil mill and manufacturing company by 1907, and finally achieved municipal incorporation in 1912 as the largest African-American town in the United States.

Isaiah T. Montgomery House

West Main Street, just off Highway 61 in Mound Bayou

Built in 1910, this two-story, red brick, Queen Anne-style house has a wide, raised porch with square Doric columns resting on brick piers, and a hipped roof with projecting gables, creating the style's typical assymetrical facade. It was built by Isaiah T. Montgomery, the founder of Mound Bayou, one of the United States's most historically and economically significant African-American settlements. The structure was recently restored by the Mississippi Department of Archives and History, thanks to a grant from the National Trust for Historic Preservation.

Isaiah Montgomery House, east elevation.

"The Delta owner of extensive lands lived, not on a farm, but on a plantation. He was known, not as a farmer, but as a planter. The word "planter". . . was a link with the antebellum past, reminiscent of the dream, if not always of the reality, of what had been."
—*David L. Cohn*

CLARKSDALE

Situated on Highway 61 at a point almost equidistant from Greenville, Greenwood, and Memphis, Clarksdale is the home of the Mississippi Blues. Fittingly, its founder John Clark, lost his father, an English architect, to a New Orleans yellow fever epidemic in 1837, leaving him alone in the world at the age of fourteen. Three years later, Clark landed at Port Royal not far from the old town of Friar's Point, near present-day Clarksdale, where he went into the logging business with a partner, Ed Porter. In 1848 he bought one hundred acres of government land for $1.25 an acre and made a fortune in cotton and lumber.

Clark's rags-to-riches story is a familiar one in Clarksdale. It was near there in 1858 that future C.S.A. Gen. Nathan Bedford Forrest, formerly a poor boy from Tennessee, acquired 3,344 acres of rich cotton land, which produced one thousand bales of cotton worth $30,000 in 1861. Almost a century later, a young man named Muddy Waters would leave his humble one-room log cabin on another Clarksdale plantation to help launch a worldwide blues revolution; a revolution that was aided by such other Clarksdale-area bluesmen as W. C. Handy, Robert Johnson, Son House, Howlin' Wolf, and John Lee Hooker. Other famous Clarksdale Horatio Alger-type stories are those of Civil Rights leader Aaron Henry, country singer Conway Twitty, New York Giants quarterback Charlie Connerly, and Lerone Bennett, Jr., executive editor of *Ebony Magazine*.

Clarksdale's unique environs and menagerie of colorful characters so intrigued Tennessee Williams, who grew up in the town's historic residential district, that the playwright used them as inspiration for many of his world-renowned plays. And today, another "local boy done good," Academy Award-winning actor Morgan Freeman, is helping to revitalize a downtown area that is as inundated with the blues as it is drenched with rich Delta history.

The Clark Mansion
211 Clark Street

Clarksdale founder John Clark began erecting this home in 1859 as a gift to his beloved wife, Eliza Alcorn Clark, the sister of future Mississippi governor and U.S. Sen. James L. Alcorn. Local legend has it that his wife, Eliza, dropped a rare and valuable steel needle through the then front porch's slats and had the porch pulled up to recover the needle. But when the Civil War broke out months later, the Pennsylvania workmen Clark had hired in order to avoid using slave labor took off for the North. Consequently, the house never had a traditional six-columned porch.

The industrious Clark nevertheless succeeded in owning and operating two steam gins, a sawmill, a lumber yard, and a general merchandise store, as well as owning stock in a cotton compress and serving as president of Clarksdale's first bank. He also jacked up his home on logs and rolled it to the present location so his daughter Blanche and her husband J. W. Cutrer could build their home on a lovely spot overlooking the Sunflower River. However, his house was laid out with the side, rather than the front, facing the street. The house is currently closed for interior renovation.

The Clark House, east elevation, has a dormered, hip roof and entry porch with slender columns in the Colonial Revival style, although the south elevation, once the house's front, was designed in the rectangular Federal style with elaborate facade pillasters, all by an unknown Pennsylvania architect.

The Cutrer Mansion
109 Clark Street

This mansion was built in 1916 by Memphis architect Bayard Cairnes for criminal attorney J. W. Cutrer and his wife Blanche Clark Cutrer, daughter of Clarksdale's founder, John Clark. The dapper Jack Cutrer was the epitome of flamboyance, equally famous for his legendary parties, fiery politics, and for shooting an 1890s newspaper reporter for alleging that one of Cutrer's forebears was of questionable lineage. Not to be outdone, Blanche often threw extravagant yard parties and opulent masked balls, usually to the accompaniment of a full orchestra or swing band. Such histrionics attracted the attention of a frequent guest in the Cutrer home, Tennessee Williams, who later based his plays, *A Streetcar Named Desire, The Glass Menagerie*, and *Cat on a Hot Tin Roof* in part on the Cutrers and their colorful Clarksdale neighbors.

The literary and architectural significance of the Cutrer House prompted Clarksdale residents, black and white, to mount a drive to save the seven-thousand-square-foot mansion from the wrecking ball in 1999, a goal accomplished when nearby Delta State University and Coahoma Community College helped raise $750,000 to purchase the home and preserve it for posterity. It is currently closed for renovation.

Cutrer Mansion, east elevation, is of the Italian Renaissance style, with a broad-roof overhang and main floor, full-length, arched windows that are more elaborate than those on the second story.

Wildberger House
104 Issaquena

This Victorian, Queen Anne-style house was built in 1898 on the site of the previous Wildberger home, which burned on Christmas Eve of 1896. It is one of Clarksdale's favorite landmarks with its two-sided, rounded porch with Eastlake-style spindlework, round tower, multiple gables, and gingerbread trim.

The private residence has never been owned by any except the Wildberger family and still features two concrete blocks at the end of the front walkway that the original Wildbergers used for mounting a horse or stepping into a carriage.

The Wildberger House, south elevation.

Madidi Restaurant
164 Delta Avenue

Originally built in 1900, this red brick structure with gaslights adorning the double, mahogany, entry doors was originally Landry's dry-goods store, where Delta planters and their wives shopped for everything from upscale clothing to fancy groceries. In 1926, the owner, Sid Landry, was struck dead by lightning on a country club golf course. The structure later housed a furniture store and was recently reopened as a restaurant by local attorney Bill Luckett and Delta native and Academy Award-winning actor Morgan Freeman.

Named for a Bolivian nature park, Madidi's French cuisine offers a local flair with such entrees as oven roasted hybrid bass, and appetizers such as catfish cakes and cornmeal-fried oysters.

Madidi, southeast elevation.

ENDURING DELTA INFLUENCE

Ole Miss (The University of Mississippi)

Although Tunica's Las Vegas-style casinos just off Highway 61, south of Memphis, signal the northernmost point of the Yazoo-Mississippi Delta, most Deltonians insist that their storied region extends all the way to the lobby of Memphis's grand old Peabody Hotel. Deltonians of 1950s and 1960s Ole Miss vintage certainly remember kicking off each of their six-era SEC football championship seasons with "Hoddy Toddy" cheers in that delightful river city hotel's lobby.

Many Ole Miss quarterbacks of Sugar Bowl-bound Rebel teams hailed from the Delta, including Archie Manning (Drew), Jimmy Lear (Greenwood), Charlie Connerly and Bobby Ray Franklin (Clarksdale), and Jimmy Heidel (Yazoo City). So did many of Ole Miss's All-America running backs—Parker Hall (Tunica), Showboat Boykin and Bobby Crespino (Greenville), and Junie Hovious (Vicksburg).

A host of Delta planters' sons and daughters attended Ole Miss, one of the earliest being Gen. Nathan Bedford Forrest's son, Willie. Yazoo City native Willie Morris served the University as writer-in-residence for many years, and Oxford's Nobel Laureate William Faulkner set many of his renowned fables in the lush, Delta woodlands. The list of Delta governors, U.S. senators, and other prominent lawyers, doctors, politicians, and business people who graduated from Ole Miss and later made significant contributions to the institution is too long for inclusion here. Suffice it to say, the Delta has cast a long shadow over Mississippi's flagship university, even though Ole Miss is located an hour away from Clarksdale in the hills of Lafayette County.

Lyceum Building
The Loop, Ole Miss Campus

Architect William Nichols completed the Lyceum Building in 1848, the year Ole Miss officially opened its doors. North and south wings were added in 1903; a facade was added to the west elevation in 1923; and the Class of 1927 donated the front facade's clock. The university recently expended $11 million to renovate this red brick structure, internationally famous for its massive, pedimented portico and six robust, supporting Ionic columns. The unadorned friezes, horizontal transom above the front entrance, and square-headed windows add substance to the classical style of this imposing structure.

The Lyceum Building, east elevation, was designed by the same architect who built Jackson's Old Capitol Museum in 1839, which once served as Mississippi's state capitol.

Barnard Observatory

Sorority Row, Ole Miss campus

Barnard Observatory, built in 1857 under the auspices of Chancellor Frederick A. P. Barnard, is one of three surviving antebellum structures on the Ole Miss campus. It was constructed as a near replica of Russia's Pulkova Observatory (b. 1839), which was destroyed during World War II. Barnard was never used as an observatory, however, because the outbreak of the Civil War prevented delivery of a nineteen-inch lens, then the largest in the world. During the war the building was used as a hospital and morgue and was spared destruction by Union forces thanks to Chancellor Barnard's acquaintance with Gen. William T. Sherman.

This Greek Revival building has housed numerous university departments and one sorority (1907-1971) but is now home to the prestigious Center for the Study of Southern Culture. It is listed on the National Register of Historic Places (1979).

Barnard Observatory, east elevation.

Rowan Oak (William Faulkner's Home)
Garfield at Old Taylor Road, Oxford

Built by Irish planter Colonel Robert Shegog in 1840, this primitive, Greek Revival-style home was purchased by future Nobel Prize-winning author William Faulkner in 1930, who named it Rowan Oak after a Scottish legend. Unable to afford necessary renovations for this center-hall plan, two-story clapboard building, Faulkner performed much of the work himself, including replacing the porch's wood floor with brick, adding a roof, and installing a balustraded brick terrace at either side of the front portico.

While residing at Rowan Oak, Faulkner penned most of his twenty-nine books, including the novels *The Sound and the Fury* (1929), *As I Lay Dying* (1930), *Light in August* (1932), *Absalom, Absalom!* (1936), and *The Reivers* (1962), which garnered him much-deserved international acclaim. The author set several of his stories in the Delta, including the short stories, "The Bear" and "Delta Autumn", and the Pulitzer Prize-winning novel, *A Fable* (1954), the outline for which is scribbled on the first floor office wall.

Rowan Oak, west elevation, is now maintained by the University of Mississippi and is listed on the National Register of Historic Places (1968).

91

Ventress Hall

The Loop, Ole Miss Campus

Ventress Hall once housed a library (1989), law school (1911), geology (1930) and art (1970) departments and is currently home to the College of Liberal Arts. It is of Romanesque Revival style as indicated by its round stone arches, gable roofs, and circular turrets, one of which stands four stories high. William Faulkner agreed to paint the turrets during the 1920s in return for being allowed to take college courses without having first graduated high school.

The interior is notable for its stained-glass window, designed by Tiffany Glass Company in New York, a memorial to the University Grays. That regiment of Ole Miss students and professors reached the high water mark of the Confederacy by breaching the stone wall near Brian's Barn at Cemetery Ridge during the Battle of Gettysburg.

Ventress Hall, south elevation.

HOLLY SPRINGS

Not all of the mansions built or maintained by Delta cotton money were erected in the Delta. The region's flood of white gold also washed over the hills of northeast Mississippi, leaving many of Mississippi's grandest homes standing in its wake. One of these was Malmaison, Choctaw Chief Greenwood Leflore's opulent Carroll County mansion, which burned to the ground in 1942. Another was Walter Place, a veritable castle of a home located in the heart of Holly Springs.

Situated on Highway 7 almost directly between Oxford and Memphis, Holly Springs was Chickasaw Indian land until 1830s cessions paved the way for incorporation in 1836. The small town has been home to at least thirteen generals, one admiral, six U.S. senators, ten U.S. congressmen, twenty judges, seven authors, and several artists. It is also the site of a key Civil War battle, sixty-four antebellum homes, and several historic churches.

First Presbyterian Church, 164 S. Memphis Street, south elevation, was built in 1860 in the Romanesque Revival style. Of special interest are the rounded brick steps, rare Bohemian grisaille-glass windows, and the bullet imbedded in the pine wood floor, left by Yankee soldiers who used the church for target practice during the town's Union occupation.

Walter Place

331 Chulahoma Avenue

Desirous of building a truly unique Southern mansion, lawyer, teacher, and businessman Harvey Washington Walter erected a home with Greek and Early Classical Revival features, including an imposing, fanlighted pediment and a portico supported by four, towering Corinthian columns, but also added battlemented octagonal towers on both ends of the structure. These two Gothic Revival towers not only made the mansion architecturally unique, but also provided much-needed space for the Walters' ten children. Walter and his three sons died of yellow fever in 1878.

In 1862, the mansion was occupied by Gen. Ulysses S. Grant and his wife Julia. Local legend has it that when Confederates later raided Holly Springs, General Van Dorn's gallant reluctance to intrude upon Mrs. Grant's privacy allowed her to hold on to her husband's important private papers. Grant repaid the courtesy by ordering the home off-limits to thieving Union soldiers on pain of death.

Walter Place, south elevation, was restored by Harvey Walter's daughters—in 1901 by Irene, after she married wealthy shoe manufacturer Oscar Johnson and again in 1933 by Annie, whose husband owned a Mississippi Delta plantation.

Sixteen-foot-high ceilings, a carpet from Agra, India, and a set of 1820 Federal chairs (right) distinguish the parlor. The dining room, viewed through the pocket doors (left), features an original Waterford chandelier and American Empire mahogany table.

A ming vase sits in an entry-hall niche above a graceful spiral staircase. The original spiral staircase was removed in 1901, but Irene Walter Johnson purchased the mansion in 1933, ripped out the "welcoming arms" staircase, and installed this spiral one.

Colonel Walter's bed is the only one original to the mansion and was likely used by General and Mrs. Grant during the Union occupation. The ten-foot-tall headboard looks smaller by virtue of the room's fourteen-foot ceiling.

This tower study is the only octagonal room in Walter Place. Grant used it as his office and probably issued his infamous, anti-Semitic Edict 11 from here, which got him in hot water with President Lincoln.